# PRAYERS FOR ALL OCCASIONS

FROM THE NATIONAL SHRINE OF
THE IMMACULATE CONCEPTION

Michigan Avenue & Fourth Street, Northeast
Washington, D.C.

*Nihil Obstat:*
Very Rev. John A. Farren, O.P.
Censor Deputatus

*Imprimatur:*
✠ James Cardinal Hickey
Archbishop of Washington
January 3, 1991

# ACKNOWLEDGEMENTS

Excerpts from the English translation of *Rite of Holy Week* © 1972, International Committee on English in the Liturgy, Inc. (ICEL); excerpts from the English translation of *The Roman Missal* © 1973, ICEL; excerpts from the English translation of *A Book of Prayers* © 1982, ICEL; excerpts from the English translation of *Order of Christian Funerals* © 1985, ICEL; excerpts from the English translation of *Book of Blessings* © 1988, ICEL. All rights reserved.

Excerpts from *Book of Blessings* © 1988, United States Catholic Conference, used with permission.

Scripture quotes from *The New American Bible* © 1970, Confraternity of Christian Doctrine, Washington, D.C., used with permission.

Prayer for Martin Luther King's Birthday, © The Liturgical Conference, 1017 12th Street, N.W., Washington, D.C. 20005. All rights reserved. Used with permission.

Printed in the United States of America.
First edition.
Cover Art: Jon Milburn.
Art of Mary, Queen of Ireland: Frank Kelly.

*My spirit rejoices
in God my Savior.*

# TABLE OF CONTENTS

# FOREWORD

Dear Friend:

The National Shrine of the Immaculate Conception was built through the prayers and support of America's Catholics to increase honor to Mary, the holy Mother of Jesus. Today, this magnificent edifice serves as a place of prayer and pilgrimage for hundreds of thousands of visitors each year. The National Shrine is not a parish church; every Catholic belongs to the Shrine family.

I encourage everyone to visit the Shrine, and pray that all our visitors will be drawn closer to God and inspired by pondering the life of Immaculate Mary.

To increase the Shrine's ministry to friends around the nation, this book of prayers was compiled to supplement your prayers and personal devotions. The book contains traditional prayers, prayers to the Saints, Marian prayers, prayers for our national holidays, prayers from the many chapels of The National Shrine, and more. I hope that you will use the book when you pray and that you will receive God's blessing in return.

If you have never visited The National Shrine, I invite you to come share in this great tribute to Mary built by America's Catholics. I promise that you will be uplifted. If you have visited the Shrine before, I encourage you to make the pilgrimage again. I ask that you remember the Shrine and its ministry in your prayers and, please, enjoy the book.

Sincerely in Christ,

Rev. Msgr. Michael J. Bransfield
Director

# INTRODUCTION

*by Michael P. Warsaw*

### The National Shrine
### of the Immaculate Conception:
### America's Church

Devotion to Mary, the Mother of Jesus, is a major element in the Catholic Heritage which was brought to this land by people from the four corners of the earth. The National Shrine of the Immaculate Conception is our nation's tribute to Mary. It honors her under the title of the Immaculate Conception, recalling that because of her unique role in salvation, Mary was free from the stain of original sin from the first moment of her conception. The National Shrine stands in recognition of the great love which America's Catholics have long held for the Immaculate Mother of God.

America's relationship with Mary began centuries ago, when Christopher Columbus sailed to the New World aboard the Santa Maria. In 1792, John Carroll, the first Catholic bishop of the United States, declared the young nation to be under Mary's protection. National devotion to Mary was further recognized at the sixth provincial Council of Baltimore in 1846. At that meeting the nation's bishops petitioned the Holy See to name Mary as the patroness of the land. The following year, Pope Pius IX granted their request and named Mary, under the title of her Immaculate Conception, as Patroness of the United States.

In the early 1900s, Bishop Thomas J. Shahan, the fourth rector of the Catholic University of America, suggested building a national shrine to Mary on the university campus in Washington. On August 15, 1913, Shahan presented his plan to Pope Pius X during a private audience in Rome. The Holy Father enthusiastically endorsed the Shrine project, making a personal contribution of four hundred dollars and calling upon the Catholics of America to support the cause. The long journey toward the completion of a national spiritual center was underway.

Upon his return from Rome, Shahan set out to make the concept of the National Shrine of the Immaculate Conception a reality. He convinced the Board of Trustees of Catholic University to donate a parcel of land at the southwest corner of the campus. Shahan then interested Catholic women's groups across the country in the proposal and enlisted their help in collecting funds for the construction of the church.

In January of 1914, Shahan published the first issue of a magazine called *Salve Regina*. It was through the pages of this small publication that Bishop Shahan built enthusiasm for the Shrine and reported on its progress. In that first issue, he wrote of his dream of "a monument of love and gratitude, a great hymn in stone . . . as perfect as the art of man can make it and as holy as the intentions of its builders could wish it to be." Nationwide support for the Shrine began to pour in. Contributions and letters of encouragement were received from every part of the country. Soon it became necessary for Shahan to have assistance in carrying out the project. Father Bernard McKenna, a priest of the Archdiocese of Philadelphia, was named the first Director of the National Shrine in 1915. Together, Shahan and McKenna labored to build the Shrine.

By 1919, architectural drawings for the Shrine had been commissioned. The noted Boston architect Charles D. Maginnis, Jr. was chosen for the work. He was assisted by Frederick V. Murphy, a Professor of Architecture at Catholic University. The first designs for the Shrine called for a gothic structure, but these were later rejected in favor of a Byzantine-Romanesque plan. This style, it was felt, was more suited to the architecture of the nation's capital and had a spiritual quality in keeping with the best tradition of church art and architecture. Early in 1920, with architectural plans completed and sufficient funds available, the decision was made to begin construction.

In May 1920, Archbishop Giovanni Bonzano, the Apostolic Delegate to the United States, blessed the site of the future Shrine at an outdoor Mass. A few months later, on September 23, 1920, James Cardinal Gibbons, the Archbishop of Baltimore, laid the cornerstone of the National Shrine.

Construction of the Crypt Church took place between 1922 and 1926, with the remainder of the Crypt level being finished in 1931. However, the Shrine's ministry did not wait for a completed structure. As early as 1923, confessions were being heard in a temporary chapel at the north end of the Crypt. The first Mass celebrated in the National Shrine took place on Easter Sunday, 1924.

Following the Great Depression of 1929, contributions to the building project slowed and with the death of Bishop Shahan in March of 1932, construction was brought to a halt. The National Shrine was to wait nearly twenty-five years for a new champion.

After the Second World War, Archbishop John Noll of Fort Wayne, Indiana, sought to revive interest in the project. Through his sermons and writings, Noll argued for the completion of the Shrine. He was joined by Archbishop Patrick O'Boyle of Washington, D.C., and together, the two worked tirelessly to rescue the dream of the National Shrine.

In 1953, the nation's Catholic bishops pledged to raise the funds needed for the construction of the Great Upper Church. Millions of people from every parish in the country contributed to the cause. Through the extraordinary generosity of America's Catholics, construction of the National Shrine of the Immaculate Conception was resumed during the Marian Year of 1954.

The contract for the building was awarded to the John McShain Company of Philadelphia, builders of such Washington landmarks as the Pentagon and the Jefferson Memorial. The work was now under the supervision of architect Eugene F. Kennedy, Jr. who had become the senior member of the firm of Maginnis and Walsh. The Shrine's superstructure rose quickly. While many of the world's great cathedrals took centuries to build, the Great Upper Church was built in less than five years.

Although some exterior work and much interior ornamentation remained to be completed, the Great Upper Church was dedicated on November 20, 1959, by Francis Cardinal Spellman, the Archbishop of New York. In the decades which followed, the many chapels and magnificent artwork of the Shrine were added.

In each of its chapels, and in the stained glass, mosaic, and sculpture of the National Shrine of the Immaculate Conception, America's heritage of devotion to Mary is recorded. More than just a magnificent building, it is a living testimony to the place the Mother of God holds in the hearts and religious life of American Catholics.

## A Place of Pilgrimage and Prayer

When Bishop Thomas Shahan first proposed the idea of a great national shrine to honor Mary, he envisioned far more than just a beautiful building adorned with the best of mosaics, sculpture, stained glass and art. His was a vision of a place of pilgrimage and prayer unique among all others in the United States. It was a dream of a church which would be a symbol of Catholicism for the nation and for the world. It was to be a reflection of the love and devotion which America's Catholics had long held for the Mother of God.

Today, many decades after Bishop Shahan first wrote of his dream of a "great hymn in stone," the National Shrine of the Immaculate Conception stands as the realization of all that he had foreseen.

The "hymn" of which Shahan once wrote resounds throughout the Shrine, even in the most silent of moments. It is heard in each of the chapels, which sing of generations of American Catholics whose faith was their strength. It has been heard on the lips of the countless millions of people who have passed through the doors of the Shrine from the earliest days of its existence. That hymn is heard from those who continue to journey to the Shrine each day.

The National Shrine proclaims the story of faith. It is the faith of people of distant lands and ancient times, and of the heritage of Christianity that has been passed from age to age. It was that heritage which was brought to America by waves of immigrants, and it is that story which they and their descendants have chosen to tell with the Shrine.

In the celebration of the Eucharist, through the Sacrament of Penance, and in the many devotions which occur daily at the Shrine, the faith of the Church is lived out, and passed on to new generations. This is the unique mission of the National Shrine of the Immaculate Conception. It has no parish community of its own; but rather, counts every American Catholic among its numbers. No single bishop claims it as his cathedral; it is the church of all of the nation's bishops. Its work is not supported by a single group or organization, but is carried out through the cooperation of people across the country. In every way, the National Shrine is America's church.

As a spiritual center for the nation, the Shrine is the destination of pilgrimages both large and small. From every state in the union, people are drawn to the Shrine in search of a renewed devotion to Christ and his Mother, Mary. Whether as part of a group or as an individual, each pilgrim comes seeking an experience of faith. Both at public worship and in times of quiet prayer, the Shrine affords an opportunity to enter into a deeper relationship with God. No one passes through the National Shrine of the Immaculate Conception without being touched by the spirit of prayer which is found within it. No one can leave its grounds without pausing for a moment to reflect upon its message, and to consider how their lives have been touched by the Shrine.

The National Shrine is an impressive place. It is impressive, not simply because of its tremendous size and beauty, but even more so because it is a house of prayer. The physical structure of the Shrine is not yet fully complete, nor is the story of faith which it tells. Built as a church for the ages, the Shrine awaits future generations of American Catholics who one day will add to that story. They will join their voices with all who have gone before them in the "great hymn in stone" that is the National Shrine of the Immaculate Conception.

# MARIAN

# PRAYERS

# THE ANGELUS

V. The angel spoke God's message to Mary,
R. and she conceived of the Holy Spirit.
Hail, Mary. . . .

V. "I am the lowly servant of the Lord:
R. let it be done to me according to your word."
Hail, Mary. . . .

V. And the Word became flesh
R. and lived among us.
Hail, Mary. . . .

V. Pray for us, holy Mother of God,
R. that we may become worthy of the promises
   of Christ.

Let us pray.

Lord,
fill our hearts with your grace:
once, through the message of an angel
you revealed to us the incarnation of your Son;
now, through his suffering and death
lead us to the glory of his resurrection.

We ask this through Christ our Lord.
R. Amen.

## HAIL, MARY

Hail Mary, full of grace
the Lord is with you!
Blessed are you among women,
and blessed is the fruit of your womb, Jesus.
Holy Mary, mother of God,
pray for us sinners,
now and at the hour of our death.
R. Amen.

## MEMORARE

Remember, most loving Virgin Mary,
never was it heard
that anyone who turned to you for help
was left unaided.

Inspired by this confidence,
though burdened by my sins,
I run to your protection
for you are my mother.

Mother of the Word of God,
do not despise my words of pleading
but be merciful and hear my prayer.
R. Amen.

## IMMACULATE CONCEPTION

We praise you, Lord,
in this daughter of Israel,
Mary, your faithful one and our mother.

We pray as she did:
may your name be holy;
may the hungry be filled and the rich know hunger;
may the proud be scattered and the oppressed raised up;
may your love be ever with your people.

We make our prayer always through Mary's child;
he arose from her the sun of justice,
Jesus, who is Lord for ever and ever.
R. Amen.

O Mary, conceived without sin,
pray for us who have recourse to you.

# THE MAGNIFICAT (CANTICLE OF MARY)

+ My soul proclaims the greatness of the Lord,
my spirit rejoices in God my Savior;
for he has looked with favor on his lowly
    servant.

From this day all generations will call me blessed:
the Almighty has done great things for me,
and holy is his Name.

He has mercy on those who fear him
in every generation.

He has shown the strength of his arm,
he has scattered the proud in their conceit.

He has cast down the mighty from their thrones,
and has lifted up the lowly.

He has filled the hungry with good things,
and the rich he has sent away empty.

He has come to the help of his servant Israel
for he has remembered his promise of mercy,
the promise he made to our fathers,
to Abraham and his children for ever.
                    *Luke 1:46–55 (Magnificat)*

## HAIL, HOLY QUEEN
## (SALVE, REGINA)

Hail, holy Queen, Mother of mercy; hail our life, our sweetness and our hope. To you do we cry, poor banished children of Eve. To you do we send up our sighs, mourning and weeping in this valley of tears. Turn then, most gracious Advocate, your eyes of mercy toward us. And after this our exile show unto us the blessed fruit of your womb, Jesus. O clement, O loving, O sweet Virgin Mary.

# AN ACT OF CONSECRATION

Most Holy Trinity: Our Father in Heaven, who chose Mary as the fairest of your daughters; Holy Spirit, who chose Mary as your spouse; God the Son, who chose Mary as your Mother; in union with Mary, we adore your majesty and acknowledge your supreme eternal dominion and authority.

Most Holy Trinity, we put the United States of America into the hands of Mary Immaculate in order that she may present the country to you. Through her we wish to thank you for the great resources of this land and for the freedom which has been its heritage. Through the intercession of Mary, have mercy on the Catholic Church in America. Grant us peace. Have mercy on our President and on all the officers of our government. Grant us a fruitful economy born of justice and charity. Have mercy on capital and industry and labor. Protect the family life of the nation. Guard the innocence of our children. Grant the precious gift of many religious vocations. Through the intercession of our Mother, have mercy on the sick, the poor, the tempted, sinners—on all who are in need.

Mary, Immaculate Virgin, Our Mother, Patroness of our land, we praise you and honor you and give ourselves to you. Protect us from every harm. Pray for us, that acting always according to your will and the Will of your Divine Son, we may live and die pleasing to God.

# LITANY OF THE BLESSED VIRGIN MARY

| | |
|---|---|
| Lord, have mercy | *Lord, have mercy* |
| Christ, have mercy | *Christ, have mercy* |
| Lord, have mercy | *Lord, have mercy* |

| | |
|---|---|
| God our Father in heaven | *have mercy on us* |
| God the Son, Redeemer of the world | *have mercy on us* |
| God the Holy Spirit | *have mercy on us* |
| Holy Trinity, one God | *have mercy on us* |

| | |
|---|---|
| Holy Mary | *pray for us* |
| Holy Mother of God | |
| Most honored of virgins | |

| | |
|---|---|
| Mother of Christ | *pray for us* |
| Mother of the Church | |
| Mother of divine grace | |
| Mother most pure | |
| Mother of chaste love | |
| Mother and virgin | |
| Sinless Mother | |
| Dearest of mothers | |

Model of motherhood                    *pray for us*
Mother of good counsel
Mother of our Creator
Mother of our Savior
Virgin most wise
Virgin rightly praised
Virgin rightly renowned
Virgin most powerful
Virgin gentle in mercy

Faithful Virgin                        *pray for us*
Mirror of justice
Throne of wisdom
Cause of our joy

Shrine of the Spirit                   *pray for us*
Glory of Israel
Vessel of selfless devotion
Mystical Rose
Tower of David
Tower of ivory
House of gold
Ark of the covenant
Gate of heaven
Morning Star
Health of the sick
Refuge of sinners
Comfort of the troubled
Help of Christians

Queen of angels                         *pray for us*
Queen of patriarchs and prophets
Queen of apostles and martyrs
Queen of confessors and virgins
Queen of all saints
Queen conceived without original sin
Queen assumed into heaven
Queen of the rosary
Queen of peace

Lamb of God, you take away
    the sins of the world          *have mercy on us*
Lamb of God, you take away
    the sins of the world          *have mercy on us*
Lamb of God, you take away
    the sins of the world          *have mercy on us*

Pray for us, holy Mother of God.
That we may become worthy of the promises of Christ.

Eternal God,
let your people enjoy constant
    health in mind and body.
Through the intercession of the Virgin Mary
free us from the sorrows of this life
and lead us to happiness in the life to come.

Grant this through Christ our Lord.

Amen.

# HOW TO PRAY THE ROSARY

(1) While holding the Crucifix in the hand, recite the Apostles' Creed.
(2) On the first bead, recite the Our Father.
(3) On the three small beads recite the Hail Mary for an increase of faith, hope and charity.
(4) Recite the Glory be to the Father.
(5) Call to mind the first Mystery and reflect upon it; then recite on the large bead the Our Father.
(6) On the ten small beads, recite the Hail Mary, keeping in mind the mystery.
(7) Recite the Glory be to the Father.
Each of the following decades continues as in the first: recall the Mystery, then say the Our Father, the ten Hail Marys and the Glory be to the Father.

# PRAYERS OF THE ROSARY

## The Apostles' Creed

I believe in God, the Father Almighty, Creator of heaven and earth; and in Jesus Christ, His only Son, our Lord; Who was conceived by the Holy Spirit, born of the Virgin Mary, suffered under Pontius Pilate, was crucified, died, and was buried. He descended into hell; the third day He rose again from the dead; He ascended into heaven, sits at the right hand of God, the Father Almighty; from thence He shall come to judge the living and the dead. I believe in the Holy Spirit, the holy Catholic Church, the communion of Saints, the forgiveness of sins, the resurrection of the body, and life everlasting. Amen.

## Our Father

Our Father, who art in heaven, hallowed be thy name; thy kingdom come; thy will be done on earth, as it is in heaven. Give us this day our daily bread; and forgive us our trespasses, as we forgive those who trespass against us; and lead us not into temptation, but deliver us from evil. Amen.

## Hail Mary

Hail Mary, full of grace; the Lord is with thee;
blessed art thou among women, and blessed is the
fruit of thy womb, Jesus. Holy Mary, Mother of
God, pray for us sinners, now and at the hour of our
death. Amen.

### Glory be to the Father

Glory be to the Father, and to the Son, and to the
Holy Spirit. As it was in the beginning, is now, and
ever shall be, world without end. Amen.

## THE JOYFUL MYSTERIES
(Monday and Thursday)

**1. The Annunciation**
"Mary said: 'I am the servant of the Lord. Let it
be done to me as you say.' "                Lk. 1:38

**2. The Visitation**
"Mary set out proceeding in haste into the hill
country to a town of Judah, where she entered
Zechariah's house and greeted Elizabeth."    Lk. 1:39

**3. The Nativity**
"She gave birth to her first-born son and wrapped
him in swaddling clothes and laid him in a manger."
                                            Lk. 2:7

**4. The Presentation**
"When the day came to purify them according to
the law of Moses, the couple brought him up to
Jerusalem so that he could be presented to the
Lord."                                      Lk. 2:22

**5. The Finding of Our Lord in the Temple**
"Son, why have you done this to us? You see that
your father and I have been searching for you in
sorrow."                                    Lk. 2:48

## THE SORROWFUL MYSTERIES
(Tuesday and Friday)

**1. The Agony of Our Lord in the Garden**
"My Father, if it is possible, let this cup pass me by. Still, let it be done as you would have it, not as I." Mt. 26:39

**2. The Scourging at the Pillar**
"Jesus he first had scourged; then he handed him over to be crucified." Mt. 27:26

**3. The Crowning with Thorns**
"They wove a crown of thorns and put it on him, and began to salute him, 'All hail! King of the Jews.' " Mk. 15:17-18

**4. The Carrying of the Cross**
"Jesus was led away, carrying the cross by himself." Jn. 19:17

**5. The Crucifixion and Death of Our Lord**
"Father, into Your hands I commend my spirit." Lk. 23:46

## THE GLORIOUS MYSTERIES
(Sunday, Wednesday and Saturday)

**1. The Resurrection**
"He has been raised up, he is not here."   Mk. 16:6

**2. The Ascension**
"The Lord Jesus was taken up into heaven."
Mk. 16:19.

**3. The Coming of the Holy Spirit**
"All were filled with the Holy Spirit."      Acts 2:4

**4. The Assumption of Mary into Heaven**
"Who is this that comes forth like the dawn?"
Song of Songs 6:10

**5. The Coronation of Mary**
"A woman clothed with the sun, on her head, a
crown of twelve stars."            Apocalypse 12:1

# CONCLUDING PRAYERS OF THE ROSARY

## Hail, Holy Queen

Hail, holy Queen, Mother of mercy; hail our life, our sweetness and our hope. To you do we cry, poor banished children of Eve. To you do we send up our sighs, mourning and weeping in this valley of tears. Turn then, most gracious Advocate, your eyes of mercy toward us. And after this our exile show unto us the blessed fruit of your womb, Jesus. O clement, O loving, O sweet Virgin Mary.

V. Pray for us, O holy Mother of God.

R. That we may become worthy of the promises of Christ.

## Let Us Pray

Let us pray. O God, by the life, death and resurrection of Your only-begotten Son, You purchased for us the rewards of eternal life; grant, we beseech you, that while meditating on these mysteries of the Holy Rosary, we may imitate what they contain and obtain what they promise. Through the same Christ our Lord. Amen.

# PRAYERS

# TO THE

# SAINTS

## PRAYER TO ST. JOSEPH

O Blessed Saint Joseph, faithful guardian and protector of virgins, to whom God entrusted Jesus and Mary, I implore you by the love which you did bear them, to preserve me from every defilement of soul and body, that I may always serve them in holiness and purity of love. Amen.

## LITANY OF ST. JOSEPH

Lord, have mercy.
Christ, have mercy.
Lord, have mercy.
Christ, hear us.
Christ, graciously hear us.
God, the Father of Heaven, *have mercy on us.*
God, the Son, Redeemer of the world, *have mercy on us.*
God the Holy Spirit, *have mercy on us.*
Holy Trinity, One God, *have mercy on us.*
Holy Mary, *pray for us.**
St. Joseph,
Renowned offspring of David,
Light of Patriarchs,
Spouse of the Mother of God,
Chaste guardian of the Virgin,
Foster father of the Son of God,
Diligent protector of Christ,
Head of the Holy Family,
Joseph most just,
Joseph most chaste,
Joseph most prudent,
Joseph most strong,
Joseph most obedient,

**Pray for us* is repeated after each invocation.

Joseph most faithful,
Mirror of patience,
Lover of poverty,
Model of artisans,
Glory of home life,
Guardian of virgins,
Pillar of families,
Solace of the wretched,
Hope of the sick,
Patron of the dying,
Terror of demons,
Protector of Holy Church,
Lamb of God, who take away the sins of the world,
   *spare us, O Lord!*
Lamb of God, who take away the sins of the world,
   *graciously hear us, O Lord!*
Lamb of God, who take away the sins of the world,
   *have mercy on us.*
V. He made him the lord of his household.
R. And prince over all his possessions.

*Let us pray.* O God, in your ineffable providence you
were pleased to choose Blessed Joseph to be the
spouse of your most holy Mother; grant, we beg
you, that we may be worthy to have him for our
intercessor in heaven whom on earth we venerate as
our Protector: You who live and reign forever and
ever.

R. Amen.

## PRAYER OF ST. FRANCIS

Lord, make me an instrument of your peace:
where there is hatred, let me sow love;
where there is injury, pardon;
where there is doubt, faith;
where there is despair, hope;
where there is darkness, light;
where there is sadness, joy.

O divine Master, grant that I may not so much seek
to be consoled as to console,
to be understood as to understand,
to be loved as to love.
For it is in giving that we receive,
it is in pardoning that we are pardoned,
it is in dying that we are born to eternal life.
R. Amen.

## PRAYER TO ST. MICHAEL

Saint Michael, the Archangel, defend us in battle; be our defense against the wickedness and snares of the devil. May God rebuke him, we humbly pray; and do you, O Prince of the heavenly host, by the power of God, thrust into hell Satan and the other evil spirits who prowl about the world for the ruin of souls. Amen.

## ST. PATRICK'S BREASTPLATE

Christ be with me, Christ within me,
Christ behind me, Christ before me,
Christ beside me, Christ to win me,
Christ to comfort and restore me,
Christ beneath me, Christ above me,
Christ in quiet, Christ in danger,
Christ in hearts of all that love me,
Christ in mouth of friend and stranger.

## PRAYER TO ST. ANN

Good Saint Ann, obtain for me an increase of faith in the great mystery of the Holy Eucharist. Help me to see in this great Sacrament Christ our High Priest, making real for me the saving grace of His death on the cross; feeding my soul with His Flesh and Blood so that I may live in Him and He in me; producing the unity of the people of God and gathering His Church together. By your powerful intercession with God, help me to center my life around the altar that I may inherit the promise of The Lord: "He who eats my flesh and drinks my blood, has life everlasting." Amen.

# PRAYER TO ST. JOHN NEUMANN

Merciful Father, You have given me all that I have in this world, even life itself. In all my daily needs, help me to remember the needs of others too. Make me aware of the need to pray to You not just for myself but for the Church, the Pope, for the clergy and for people who suffer any need.

Make me as selfless as Saint John Neumann was. Throughout my life, give me the grace to direct my first thoughts to the service of You and of others. Make my prayer—"Your will be done" knowing that in Your mercy and love, Your will for me is my sanctification. I ask this through Jesus Christ, our Lord. Amen.

## PRAYER TO ST. JUDE

St. Jude, glorious apostle, faithful servant and friend of Jesus, the name of the traitor has caused you to be forgotten by many, but the true Church invokes you universally as the Patron of things despaired of; pray for me, who am so miserable; pray for me that finally I may receive the consolations and the succor of Heaven in all my necessities, tribulations and sufferings, particularly (here make your request), and that I may bless God with the Elect throughout Eternity. Amen.

## PRAYER TO ST. ANTHONY

O Holy St. Anthony, gentlest of Saints, your love for God and charity for His creatures, made you worthy, when on earth, to possess miraculous powers. Miracles waited on your word, which you were ever ready to speak for those in trouble or anxiety. Encouraged by this thought, I implore of you to obtain for me (request). The answer to my prayer may require a miracle; even so, you are the Saint of Miracles. O gentle and loving St. Anthony, whose heart was ever full of human sympathy, whisper my petition into the ears of the Sweet Infant Jesus, who loved to be folded in your arms; and the gratitude of my heart will be ever yours. Amen.

# TRADITIONAL
# PRAYERS

# THE LORD'S PRAYER

Our Father, who art in heaven,
hallowed be thy name;
thy kingdom come;
thy will be done on earth as it is in heaven.
Give us this day our daily bread;
and forgive us our trespasses
as we forgive those who trespass against us;
and lead us not into temptation,
but deliver us from evil.
Amen.

## APOSTLES' CREED

I believe in God, the Father almighty,
  creator of heaven and earth.
I believe in Jesus Christ, his only Son, our Lord.
  He was conceived by the power of the
    Holy Spirit
    and born of the Virgin Mary.

  He suffered under Pontius Pilate,
    was crucified, died, and was buried.
  He descended to the dead.
  On the third day he rose again.
  He ascended into heaven,
    and is seated at the right hand of the Father.
  He will come again to judge the living and the
    dead.

I believe in the Holy Spirit,
  the holy catholic Church,
  the communion of saints,
  the forgiveness of sins,
  the resurrection of the body,
  and the life everlasting.
  Amen.

## AN ACT OF CONTRITION

O my God, I am heartily sorry for having offended you, and I detest all my sins because of your just punishment. I firmly resolve, with the help of your grace, to sin no more, and to avoid the near occasions of sin. Amen.

## AN ACT OF FAITH

O my God, who are infallible Truth and can neither deceive nor be deceived, I firmly believe all that you have revealed and propose to my belief through your holy Church, because you have revealed it. I believe that you are one in nature and three in Persons: the Father, the Son, and the Holy Spirit. I believe that you are the Creator of all things and that you reward the just for all eternity in heaven and punish the wicked for all eternity in hell. I believe that Jesus Christ is the Son of God made man, that he suffered and died for my sins and rose from the dead in glory, and that it is only in him through the Holy Spirit that eternal life is given to us. I believe in all that your holy Church believes. I thank you for having called me to the true faith, and I propose that with the help of your grace I will live and die in this holy faith. Amen.

## AN ACT OF LOVE

O my God, because you are infinite goodness and worthy of infinite love, I love you with my whole heart above all things, and for love of you I love my neighbor as myself. Amen.

## AN ACT OF HOPE

O my God, trusting in your promises and because you are faithful, powerful and merciful, I hope, through the merits of Jesus Christ, for the pardon of my sins, final perseverance and the blessed glory of heaven. Amen.

## THE DIVINE PRAISES

Blessed be God.
Blessed be His Holy Name.
Blessed be Jesus Christ, true God and true man.
Blessed be the Name of Jesus.
Blessed be His Most Sacred Heart.
Blessed be His Most Precious Blood.
Blessed be Jesus in the Most Holy Sacrament of
  the Altar.
Blessed be the Holy Spirit, the Paraclete.
Blessed be the great Mother of God, Mary
  most holy.
Blessed be her holy and Immaculate Conception.
Blessed be her glorious Assumption.
Blessed be the name of Mary, Virgin and Mother.
Blessed be St. Joseph, her most chaste spouse.
Blessed be God in His angels and in His Saints.
May the heart of Jesus, in the Most Blessed
  Sacrament, be praised, adored, and loved with
  grateful affection, at every moment, in all the
  tabernacles of the world, even to the end of
  time. Amen.

## PRAYER TO THE HOLY TRINITY

Glory be to the Father,
   Who by His almighty power and love created me,
   making me in the image and likeness of God.
Glory be to the Son,
   Who by His Precious Blood delivered me from
   hell, and opened for me the gates of heaven.
Glory be to the Holy Spirit,
   Who has sanctified me in the sacrament of
   Baptism, and continues to sanctify me by the
   graces I receive daily from His bounty.
Glory be to the Three adorable Persons of the Holy
   Trinity, now and forever. Amen.

## PRAYER TO THE HOLY SPIRIT

Come, Holy Spirit,
  fill my heart with Your holy gifts.

Let my weakness be penetrated with Your strength
  this very day that I may fulfill all the duties of my
  state conscientiously, that I may do what is right
  and just.

Let my charity be such as to offend no one, and hurt
  no one's feelings; so generous as to pardon
  sincerely any wrong done to me.

Assist me, O Holy Spirit,
  in all my trials of life, enlighten me in my
  ignorance, advise me in my doubts, strengthen me
  in my weakness, help me in all my needs, protect
  me in temptations and console me in afflictions.

Graciously hear me, O Holy Spirit,
  and pour Your light into my heart, my soul, and
  my mind.

Assist me to live a holy life and to grow in goodness
  and grace. Amen.

## DAILY PRAYER
## TO THE SACRED HEART

Sacred Heart of Jesus, today I wish to live in You, in Your grace, in which I desire at all costs to persevere.

Keep me from sin and strengthen my will by helping me to keep watch over my senses, my imagination, and my heart.

Help me to correct my faults which are the source of sin.

I beg You to do this, O Jesus, through Mary, Your Immaculate Mother. Amen.

## PRAYER FOR THE
## SOULS IN PURGATORY

O gentle Heart of Jesus, ever present in the Blessed
Sacrament, ever consumed with burning love for
the poor captive souls in Purgatory, have mercy
on them.
Be not severe in Your judgments, but let some drops
of Your Precious Blood fall upon the devouring
flames.
And, Merciful Savior, send Your angels to conduct
them to a place of refreshment, light and peace.
Amen.

## PRAYER FOR A FAMILY

O dear Jesus,
  I humbly implore You to grant Your special graces
  to our family. May our home be the shrine of
  peace, purity, love, labor and faith. I beg You,
  dear Jesus, to protect and bless all of us, absent
  and present, living and dead.

O Mary,
  loving Mother of Jesus, and our Mother, pray to
  Jesus for our family, for all the families of the
  world, to guard the cradle of the newborn, the
  schools of the young and their vocations.

Blessed Saint Joseph,
  holy guardian of Jesus and Mary, assist us by your
  prayers in all necessities of life. Ask of Jesus that
  special grace which He granted to you, to watch
  over our home at the pillow of the sick and the
  dying, so that with Mary and with you, heaven
  may find our family unbroken in the Sacred Heart
  of Jesus. Amen.

## THE BEATITUDES

Blessed are the poor in spirit,
  for theirs is the kingdom of heaven.
Blessed are they who mourn,
  for they shall be comforted.
Blessed are the meek,
  for they shall possess the earth.
Blessed are they who hunger and thirst for justice,
  for they shall be satisfied.
Blessed are the merciful,
  for they shall obtain mercy.
Blessed are the clean of heart,
  for they shall see God.
Blessed are the peacemakers,
  for they shall be called children of God.
Blessed are they who suffer persecution for justice' sake,
  for theirs is the kingdom of heaven.
Blessed are you when men reproach you, and
  persecute you, and
speaking falsely, say all manner of evil against you,
  for my sake.

## PRAYER OF SOLACE

May Christ support us all the day long,
till the shadows lengthen,
and the evening comes,
and the busy world is hushed,
and the fever of life is over
and our work is done.
Then in his mercy
may he give us a safe lodging,
and holy rest and peace at the last.

Amen.

(attributed to John Cardinal Newman)

# PILGRIM'S PRAYER

O Virgin Mary, Help of Christians, we dedicate ourselves to your service. We concentrate our minds, hearts, and bodies and promise to work always for the glory of God and the salvation of all people. We pray for the Church throughout the world. Protect the young and help the aged, save sinners and console the dying. You are our hope, Mary, Mother of Mercy and Gate of Heaven. Pray to your Son for us so that we may be filled with selfless charity and deep faith. Ask Jesus for those things which we cannot obtain through our own actions and help us in this our present necessity. May we always see the Will of the Father in our lives. We ask you this, sweet Spouse of the Spirit, so that we may come to your Son in grace. Amen.

## PRAYER FOR PRIESTS

O Jesus, I pray for Your faithful and fervent priests;
for Your unfaithful and tepid priests; for Your
priests laboring at home or abroad in distant
mission fields; for Your tempted priests; for Your
lonely and desolate priests; for Your young priests;
for Your dying priests; for the souls of Your
priests in purgatory.
But above all I recommend to You the priests dearest
to me; the priest who baptized me; the priests who
absolved me from my sins; the priests at whose
Masses I assisted and who gave me Your Body and
Blood in Holy Communion; the priests who
taught and instructed me; all the priests to whom I
am indebted in any other way. O Jesus, keep them
all close to Your heart, and bless them abundantly
in time and in eternity. Amen.

## PRAYER FOR VOCATIONS

Heavenly Father, your divine Son taught us to pray to the Lord of the harvest to send laborers into His vineyard. We earnestly beg You to bless our Archdiocese and our world with many priests and religious who will love You fervently, and gladly and courageously spend their lives in service to Your Son's Church under the guidance of the Holy Spirit. We pray that their lives may be always centered on our Eucharistic Lord, that they be always faithful to the Holy Father, and that they may be devoted sons and daughters of Mary, our mother, in making You known and loved that all may attain Heaven. Bless our families, and our children and choose from our homes those whom You desire for this holy work. We ask this in Jesus' name. Amen.

## PRAYER TO CHRIST THE KING

Christ Jesus, I acknowledge You King of the universe. All that has been created has been made for You. Make full use of Your rights over me.

I renew the promises I made in Baptism, when I renounced Satan and all his pomps and works, and I promise to live a good Christian life and to do all in my power to procure the triumph of the rights of God and Your Church.

Divine Heart of Jesus, I offer you my efforts in order to obtain that all hearts may acknowledge your Sacred Royalty, and that thus the Kingdom of Your peace may be established throughout the universe. Amen.

## AT BEDSIDE

Now I lay me down to sleep,
I pray the Lord my soul to keep.
Four corners to my bed,
Four angels there aspread:
Two to foot and two to head,
And four to carry me when I'm dead.
If any danger come to me,
Sweet Jesus Christ deliver me.
And if I die before I wake,
I pray the Lord my soul to take.

Amen.

## THE SERENITY PRAYER

God grant me
Serenity to accept the things I cannot change,
Courage to change the things I can, and
Wisdom to know the difference.

# PSALM 23

The LORD is my shepherd: I shall not
  want.
In verdant pastures he gives me
  repose;
Beside restful waters he leads me;
  he refreshes my soul.
He guides me in right paths
  for his name's sake.
Even though I walk in the dark valley
  I fear no evil; for you are at my side
With your rod and your staff
  that give me courage.

You spread the table before me
  in the sight of my foes;
You anoint my head with oil;
  my cup overflows.
Only goodness and kindness follow me
  all the days of my life;
And I shall dwell in the house of the
  LORD
  for years to come.

# ANIMA CHRISTI

Soul of Christ, sanctify me.
Body of Christ, heal me.
Blood of Christ, drench me.
Water from the side of Christ, wash me.
Passion of Christ, strengthen me.

Good Jesus, hear me.

In your wounds shelter me.
From turning away keep me.
From the evil one protect me.
At the hour of me death call me.
Into your presence lead me,
to praise you with all your saints
for ever and ever.
R. Amen.

# PRAYERS FOR

# VARIOUS NEEDS

## IN THANKSGIVING FOR A FAVOR RECEIVED

Thank You, O God, for hearing my prayer and granting my request. Thank You for all the kindness You have shown me.

Thank You, Father, for Your great love in giving me my life, for Your great patience in preserving me despite my sinfulness, for Your protection in the past and for the opportunity to serve and honor You in the future.

Thank You, Lord Jesus, for keeping me numberless times from sin and death by the toils of Your life, the sufferings of Your Passion, and by Your victorious Resurrection.

Thank You, Holy Spirit of God, for bestowing so many graces upon my soul and for having so frequently renewed Your life within me.

May my life, from now on, be a sign of my greatfulness. Amen.

## BLESSING OF
## AN ADVENT WREATH

Lord God,
let your blessing come upon us
as we light the candles of this wreath.
May the wreath and its light
be a sign of Christ's promise to bring us
    salvation.
May he come quickly and not delay.

We ask this through Christ our Lord.
R. Amen.

## BLESSING OF
## A CHRISTMAS CRECHE

God of Mary and Joseph, of shepherds and
    animals,
bless us whenever we gaze on this manger
    scene.
Through all the days of Christmas
may these figures tell the story
of how humans, angels, and animals
found the Christ in this poor place.

Fill our house with hospitality, joy,
gentleness, and thanksgiving
and guide our steps in the way of peace.

Grant this through Christ our Lord.
R. Amen.

## BLESSING OF
## A CHRISTMAS TREE

God of all creation,
we praise you for this tree
which brings beauty and memories and the
   promise of life to our home.
May your blessing be upon all who gather
   around this tree,
all who keep the Christmas festival by its
   lights.
We wait for the coming of the Christ,
the days of everlasting justice and of peace.
You are our God, living and reigning, for ever
   and ever.
R. Amen.

## BLESSING FOR THE NEW YEAR

Remember us, O God;
from age to age be our comforter.
You have given us the wonder of time,
blessings in days and nights, seasons and years.

Bless your children at the turning of the year
and fill the months ahead with the bright hope
that is ours in the coming of Christ.

You are our God, living and reigning, for ever
and ever.
R. Amen.

# STATIONS OF THE CROSS

## Prayer before the Stations

My Lord Jesus Christ, You have made this journey to die for me with love unutterable, and I have so many times unworthily abandoned You; but now I love You with my whole heart, and because I love You, I repent sincerely for having ever offended You. Pardon me, my God, and permit me to accompany You on this journey. You go to die for love of me: I wish also, my beloved Redeemer, to die for love of You. My Jesus, I will always live and die united to You.

## 1. Jesus is Condemned to Death
O Jesus, help me to appreciate Your sanctifying grace more and more.

## 2. Jesus Bears His Cross
O Jesus, You chose to die for me. Help me to love You always with all my heart.

## 3. Jesus Falls the First Time
O Jesus, make me strong to conquer my wicked passions, and to rise quickly from sin.

### 4. Jesus Meets His Mother
O Jesus, grant me a tender love for Your Mother, who offered You for love of me.

### 5. Jesus is Helped by Simon
O Jesus, like Simon lead me ever closer to You through my daily crosses and trials.

### 6. Jesus and Veronica
O Jesus, imprint Your image on my heart that I may be faithful to You all my life.

### 7. Jesus Falls a Second Time
O Jesus, I repent for having offended You. Grant me forgiveness of all my sins.

### 8. Jesus Speaks to the Women
O Jesus, grant me tears of compassion for Your sufferings and of sorrow for my sins.

### 9. Jesus Falls a Third Time
O Jesus, let me never yield to despair. Let me come to You in hardship and spiritual distress.

### 10. He is Stripped of His Garments
O Jesus, let me sacrifice all my attachments rather than imperil the divine life of my soul.

### 11. Jesus is Nailed to the Cross
O Jesus, strengthen my faith and increase my love for You. Help me to accept my crosses.

### 12. Jesus Dies on the Cross
O Jesus, I thank You for making me a child of God. Help me to forgive others.

### 13. Jesus is Taken Down from the Cross
O Jesus, through the intercession of Your holy Mother, let me be pleasing to You.

### 14. Jesus is Laid in the Tomb
O Jesus, strengthen my will to live for You on earth and bring me to eternal bliss in heaven.

## Prayer after the Stations

Jesus, You became an example of humility, obedience and patience, and preceded me on the way of life bearing Your Cross. Grant that, inflamed with Your love, I may cheerfully take upon myself the sweet yoke of Your Gospel together with the mortification of the Cross and follow You as a true disciple so that I may be united with You in heaven. Amen.

## PRAYER TO
## JESUS CHRIST CRUCIFIED

My good and dear Jesus,
I kneel before you,
asking you most earnestly
to engrave upon my heart
a deep and lively
faith, hope, and charity,
with true repentance
for my sins,
and a firm resolve
to make amends.
As I reflect upon
your five wounds,
and dwell upon them with
deep compassion and grief,
I recall, good Jesus,
the words the prophet David
spoke long ago
concerning yourself:
they have pierced my hands
and my feet, they have
counted all my bones!

## THE EASTER VIGIL

Rejoice, heavenly powers! Sing, choirs of angels!
Exult, all creation around God's throne!
Jesus Christ, our King, is risen!
Sound the trumpet of salvation!

Rejoice, O earth, in shining splendor,
radiant in the brightness of your King!
Christ has conquered! Glory fill you!
Darkness vanishes for ever!

O happy fault, O necessary sin of Adam,
which gained for us so great a Redeemer!

The power of this holy night
dispels all evil, washes guilt away,
restores lost innocence, brings mourners joy;
it casts out hatred, brings us peace,
and humbles earthy pride.

Night truly blessed when heaven is wedded to
    earth
and we are reconciled with God!

*Exsultet*

Alleluia!

# PRAYER OF SPOUSES FOR EACH OTHER

Lord Jesus, grant that I and my spouse may have a true and understanding love for each other. Grant that we may both be filled with faith and trust. Give us the grace to live with each other in peace and harmony. May we always bear with one another's weaknesses and grow from each other's strengths. Help us to forgive one another's failings and grant us patience, kindness, cheerfulness and the spirit of placing the well-being of one another ahead of self.

May the love that brought us together grow and mature with each passing year. Bring us both ever closer to You through our love for each other. Let our love grow to perfection. Amen.

## BLESSING ON ANNIVERSARIES

Almighty and eternal God,
you have so exalted the unbreakable bond of
    marriage
that it has become the sacramental sign
of your Son's union with the Church as his
    spouse.

Look with favor on us whom you have
    united in marriage,
as we ask for your help
and the protection of the Virgin Mary.
We pray that in good times and in bad
we will grow in love for each other;
that we will resolve to be of one heart
in the bond of peace.

Lord, in our struggles let us rejoice
that you are near to help us;
in our needs let us know
that you are there to rescue us;
in our joys let us see
that you are the source and completion of
    every happiness.

We ask this through Christ our Lord.
R. Amen.

## PRAYER IN TIME OF SUFFERING

Behold me, my beloved Jesus, weighed down under the burden of my trials and sufferings, I cast myself at Your feet, that You may renew my strength and my courage, while I rest here in Your Presence. Permit me to lay down my cross in Your Sacred Heart, for only Your infinite goodness can sustain me; only Your love can help me bear my cross; only Your powerful hand can lighten its weight. O Divine King, Jesus, whose heart is so compassionate to the afflicted, I wish to live in You; suffer and die in You. During my life be to me my model and my support; at the hour of my death, be my hope and my refuge. Amen.

## PRAYER IN TIME OF SICKNESS

O Jesus, You suffered and died for us;
You understand suffering;
Teach me to understand my suffering as You do;
To bear it in union with You;
To offer it with You to atone for my sins
And to bring Your grace to souls in need.
Calm my fears; increase my trust.
May I gladly accept Your holy will and become
  more like You in trial.
If it be Your will, restore me to health so that
  I may work for Your honor and glory and
  the salvation of all. Amen.

## PRAYER FOR THE SICK

Dear Jesus, Divine Physician and Healer of the Sick, we turn to You in this time of illness. O dearest Comforter of the Troubled, alleviate our worry and sorrow with Your gentle love, and grant us the grace and strength to accept this burden. Dear God, we place our worries in Your hands. We place our sick under Your care and humbly ask that You restore Your servant to health again. Above all, grant us the grace to acknowledge Your holy will and know that whatsoever You do, You do for the love of us. Amen.

## PRAYERS FOR MOURNERS

Lord,
N. is gone now from this earthly dwelling,
and has left behind those who mourn his/her
    absence.
Grant that we may hold his/her memory dear,
never bitter for what we have lost
nor in regret for the past,
but always in hope of the eternal kingdom
where you will bring us together again.


We ask this through Christ our Lord.
R. Amen.

## PRAYER AT THE GRAVESIDE

Lord Jesus Christ,
by your own three days in the tomb,
you hallowed the graves of all who believe in
    you
and so made the grave a sign of hope
that promises resurrection
even as it claims our mortal bodies.

Grant that our brother/sister, N., may sleep
    here in peace
until you awaken him/her to glory,
for you are the resurrection and the life.
Then he/she will see you face to face
and in your light will see light
and know the splendor of God,
for you live and reign for ever and ever.
R. Amen.

# PRAYERS
# FOR DAYS
# OUR NATION
# CELEBRATES

## MARTIN LUTHER KING'S BIRTHDAY

Lord our God,
see how oppression and violence are our sad
   inheritance,
one generation to the next.
We look for you where the lowly are raised up,
where the mighty are brought down.
We find you there in your servants,
and we give you thanks this day
for your preacher and witness, Martin Luther
   King, Jr.
Fill us with your spirit:
where our human community is divided by
   racism,
torn by repression,
saddened by fear and ignorance,
may we give ourselves to your work of healing.

Grant this through Christ our Lord.
R. Amen.

## GEORGE WASHINGTON'S BIRTHDAY

Almighty and eternal God,
you have revealed your glory to all nations.
God of power and might, wisdom and justice,
through you authority is rightly administered,
laws are enacted, and judgment is decreed.

Assist with your spirit of counsel and fortitude
the President of these United States,
that his/her administration
    may be conducted in righteousness,
and be eminently useful to your people
    over whom he/she presides.
May he/she encourage due respect for virtue and
    religion.
May he/she execute the laws with justice and
    mercy.
May he/she seek to restrain crime, vice, and
    immorality.

We, likewise, commend to your unbounded
    mercy
all who dwell in the United States.
Bless us and all people with the peace
which the world cannot give.

We pray to you, who are Lord and God, for ever
and ever.
R. Amen.

*Archbishop John Carroll (alt.)*

## MOTHER'S DAY

Loving God
as a mother gives life and nourishment to her
    children,
so you watch over your Church.
Bless our mother.
Let the example of her faith and love shine forth.
Grant that we, her family,
may honor her always
with a spirit of profound respect.

Grant this through Christ our Lord.
R. Amen.

## FATHER'S DAY

God our Father,
in your wisdom and love you made all things.
Bless our father.
Let the example of his faith and love shine forth.
Grant that we, his family,
may honor him always
with a spirit of profound respect.

Grant this through Christ our Lord.
R. Amen.

## INDEPENDENCE DAY

God, source of all freedom,
this day is bright with the memory
of those who declared that life and liberty
are your gift to every human being.

Help us to continue a good work begun long ago.
Make our vision clear and our will strong:
that only in human solidarity will we find liberty,
and justice only in the honor that belongs
to every life on earth.

Turn our hearts toward the family of nations:
to understand the ways of others,
to offer friendship,
and to find safety only in the common good of
    all.

We ask this through Christ our Lord.
R. Amen.

## THANKSGIVING DAY

Lord, we thank you
for the goodness of our people
and for the spirit of justice
that fills this nation.
We thank you for the beauty and fullness of the
    land and the challenge of the cities.

We thank you for our work and our rest,
for one another, and for our homes.
We thank you, Lord:

*(Pause for other prayers of thanksgiving.)*

For all that we have spoken
and for all that we keep in our hearts,
accept our thanksgiving on this day.

We pray and give thanks through Jesus Christ
our Lord.
R. Amen.

# THE

# NATIONAL SHRINE

# CHAPEL PRAYERS

In response to the
many requests we receive
from visitors to The National Shrine,
the following prayers are
from the Shrine chapels.

## OUR LADY, QUEEN OF PEACE

God, our Father,
Creator of the world,
you established the order which govern all ages.
Hear our prayer and grant us peace in our time
as we rejoice in your glory
and praise you without end.

Mary, Queen of Peace, look upon us kindly.
Through your prayers
obtain for us the gift of peace
which your Son promised.

We ask this through the same Lord Jesus Christ,
Prince of Peace,
Son of God, Son of Mary,
who lives and reigns with the Father
and the Holy Spirit,
one God, forever and ever. Amen.

## OUR LADY OF LOURDES

O ever Immaculate Virgin, Mother of mercy,
health of the sick, refuge of sinners,
comforter of the afflicted,
you know my wants, my troubles,
my sufferings;
look with mercy on me.
By appearing in the Grotto of Lourdes,
you were pleased to make it a
privileged sanctuary,
whence you dispense your favors;
and already many sufferers have
obtained the cure of their infirmities,
both spiritual and corporal.
I come, therefore, with complete confidence
to implore your maternal intercession.
Obtain, O loving Mother, the grant of
my requests.
Through gratitude for your favors,
I will endeavor to imitate your virtues,
that I may one day share your glory. Amen.

## MOTHER OF GOD
### (Eastern Rites Chapel)

O Mary, Mother of God,

As you are above all creatures
in heaven and on earth,
more glorious than the Cherubim,
more noble than any here below,
Christ has given you to His people,
firm bulwark and protectress,
to shield and save sinners
who fly to you.
Therefore, O Lady,
all-embracing refuge,
we solemnly recall your sweet protection,
and beg the Christ forever for His mercy. Amen.

## OUR LADY OF BREZJE

Mary, Help of Christians, you show us
how to be Christian, how to "hear the word
of God and keep it." (Lk. 11:28). Help
us to respond to God as you did, that
His power work in us, that the Spirit
form Christ in us, and that His mind,
His heart, His will be ours.

We ask this through Christ, Our Lord. Amen.

## IMMACULATE HEART OF MARY

Father,
you prepared the heart of the Virgin Mary
to be a fitting home for your Holy Spirit.
By her prayers,
may we become more worthy temples of your glory.
Grant this through our Lord Jesus Christ,
your Son,
Who lives and reigns with you and the
Holy Spirit,
one God, for ever and ever. Amen.

## OUR LADY OF BISTRICA

Immaculate Mother of Jesus,
we honor you as God's chosen one,
beautiful, beloved, and free from all sin.
Keep watch over us,
pray that we rise above our sins and
failings and come to share the fullness of grace.
Be a mother to us in the order of grace
by assisting us to live your obedience,
your faith, your hope and your love. Amen.

## QUEEN OF MISSIONS

Holy Mary, Our Mother

Today, each day and in our last hour
    We entrust ourselves entirely to your
    loving and singular care.

We place in your hands:
    Our entire hope and happiness,
    Our every anxiety and difficulty,
    Our whole lives.

May our every endeavor be directed and guided
    according to the Will of Your Son,
    which is your will—by the aid of your
    prayer and special favor with God. Amen.

## MOTHER OF GOOD COUNSEL

We turn to you
our Mother of Good Counsel
as we seek to imitate
your faith-filled life.
May we be led by the same Wisdom
which God sent forth from heaven
to guide you along unfamiliar paths
and through challenging decisions.
Keep us united in mind and heart
as we go forward in joyful hope
toward the grace-filled freedom
that Augustine recommends.
O Virgin Mother of good counsel,
hear our prayer
as we look to you for guidance.
Pray for us
to our loving and merciful Father,
to your Son, our Lord Jesus Christ,
and to the Holy Spirit,
giver of all wisdom
one God, for ever and ever. Amen.

## MARY, HELP OF CHRISTIANS

Most Holy and Immaculate Virgin, Help of Christians, Mother of the Church, we place ourselves under your motherly protection. We promise to be faithful to our Christian vocation and to work for the greater glory of God and the salvation of our souls, and of those entrusted to us.

With faith in your intercession, we pray for the Church, for our family and friends, for youth, especially those most in need.

You were St. John Bosco's teacher. Show us how to imitate his virtues: especially his union with God, his chastity, humility, and poverty, his love for work and for temperance, his goodness and total giving of self to others, his loyalty to the Holy Father and to the Church.

Grant, O Mary, Help of Christians, the graces of which we stand in need. (Here mention your intentions.) May we serve God with fidelity and generosity until death. Help us and our dear ones to attain the boundless joy of being forever with our Father in heaven. Amen.

## OUR LADY OF CZESTOCHOWA

O Mother of God, Immaculate Mary, to Thee do I dedicate my body and soul, all my prayers and deeds, my joys and sufferings, all that I am and all that I have.

With a joyful heart I surrender myself to Thy bondage of love.

To Thee will I devote my services of my own free will for the salvation of mankind, and for the help of the Holy Church whose Mother Thou art.

From now on my only desire is to do all things with Thee, through Thee, and for Thee. I know I can accomplish nothing by my own strength, whereas Thou canst do everything that is the will of Thy Son and Thou art always victorious. Grant, therefore, O Helper of the faithful, that my family, parish, and homeland might become in truth the Kingdom where Thou reignest with Thy Son. Amen.

## OUR LADY OF GUADALUPE

Dearest Lady of Guadalupe, fruitful Mother of
Holiness, teach me your ways of gentleness and
strength. Hear my prayer, offered with
deep-felt confidence to beg this favor:...

O Mary, conceived without sin, I come to your
throne of grace to share the fervent devotion of
your faithful Mexican children who call to
thee under the glorious Aztec title of ''Guadalupe''
—the Virgin who crushed the serpent.

Queen of Martyrs, whose Immaculate Heart was
pierced by seven swords of grief, help me to
walk valiantly amid the sharp thorns strewn
across my pathway. Invoke the Holy Spirit of
Wisdom to fortify my will to frequent the
Sacraments so that, thus enlightened and
strengthened, I may prefer God to all creatures
and shun every occasion of sin.

Help me, as a living branch of the Vine that is
Jesus Christ, to exemplify His divine charity
always seeking the good of others.
Queen of Apostles, aid me to win souls for the
Sacred Heart of my Savior.
Keep my apostolate fearless, dynamic and
articulate, to proclaim the loving solitude of

Our Father in Heaven so that the wayward may heed His pleading and obtain pardon, through the merits of your merciful Son, Our Lord Jesus Christ. Amen.

## THE MIRACULOUS MEDAL

O Virgin Mother of God,
Mary Immaculate,
we dedicate and consecrate ourselves to you
under the title of Our Lady of the
Miraculous Medal.
May this Medal be for each one of us
a sure sign of your affection for us
and a constant reminder of our duties toward you.
Ever while wearing it,
may we be blessed by your loving protection
and preserved in the grace of your Son.
O Most powerful Virgin,
Mother of our Savior,
keep us close to you
every moment of our lives.
Obtain for us, your children,
the grace of a happy death;
so that, in union with you,
we may enjoy the
bliss of heaven forever. Amen.

## OUR LADY, QUEEN OF IRELAND

Holy Mary if thou wilt,
hear Thy suppliant;
I put myself under the
shelter of Thy shield.
When falling in the slippery
path Thou art my smooth
supporting hand staff.
There is no hound in
fleetness or in chase,
north wind or rapid river;
as quick as the
Mother of Christ
to the bed of death,
to those who are entitled
to her kindly protection. Amen.

## MARY, QUEEN OF ALL HEARTS

Father,
you have given us the mother of your Son
to be our queen and mother.
With the support of her prayers
may we come to share the glory of your children
in the kingdom of heaven.
We ask this through our Lord Jesus Christ,
your Son,
who lives and reigns with you and the Holy Spirit,
one God, for ever and ever. Amen.

## OUR LADY OF SILUVA

O most Holy Virgin Mary, you who appeared to the shepherds in the fields at Siluva, you whose tears bathed the rock where once an altar stood, you who with plaintive voice said: "You plow and seed here where formerly my Son was honored," grant that we, moved by your tears may once, as our forefathers did, revive the spirit of adoration of your Son in our fallow hearts, strengthen the tottering structure of the shrine which is the family, and seek forgiveness for the negligences and sins of our nation.

O Mother of God, we desire to raise up the glory of your revelation from forgotten ruins, that we may all the more honor you the patroness of our country, and, with your help, obtain for our nation the spirit of a living Faith. Through Christ our Lord. Amen.

## MOTHER OF SORROWS

Father,
as your Son was raised on the cross,
his mother Mary stood by him, sharing his suffering
May your Church be united with Christ
in his suffering and death
and so come to share in his rising to new life,
where he lives and reigns with you and the Holy Spirit,
one God, for ever and ever.

## OUR LADY OF THE ROSARY

O God, whose only-begotten Son,
by His life, death and
resurrection, has won for us
the rewards of eternal salvation,
grant, we pray,
that we, who meditate
on these mysteries
of the most holy Rosary
of the Blessed Virgin Mary,
may imitate what they contain
and obtain what they promise.
Through the same Christ our Lord. Amen.

## OUR LADY OF FATIMA

Most Holy Virgin, who hast deigned to come
to Fatima, to reveal the treasures of
graces hidden in the recitation of the Rosary,
inspire our hearts with a sincere love
of this devotion, that meditating on the
Mysteries of our Redemption recalled therein,
we may obtain the conversion of sinners,
the conversion of Russia, and the favors we
ask you now for the greater glory of God,
for your own honor, and for the good of souls.
Amen.

## MARY, MOTHER OF MANKIND
### (Memorial Hall)

Mother, I commend and entrust to you
all that goes to make up earthly progress,
asking that it should not be one-sided,
but that it should create conditions
for the full spiritual advancement of
individuals, families, communities and nations.
I commend to you the poor, the suffering,
the sick and the handicapped,
the aging and the dying.
I ask you to reconcile those in sin,
to heal those in pain, and to uplift
those who have lost their hope and joy.
Show to those who struggle in doubt the
light of Christ your Son. Amen.

## OUR LADY OF MOUNT CARMEL

O Most beautiful flower of Mount Carmel,
fruitful vine,
splendor of heaven,
Blessed Mother of the Son of God,
Immaculate Virgin,
assist me in this my necessity.
O, star of the sea,
help me
and show me herein you are my mother.

O holy Mary, Mother of God,
Queen of heaven and earth,
I humbly beseech you
from the bottom of my heart,
to succor me in this necessity;
there are none that can withstand your power.

O show me herein you are my Mother.
O Mary, conceived without sin,
pray for us
who have recourse to thee *(three times)*.

Sweet Mother, I place this cause in your hands
*(three times)*.

# MOTHER OF PERPETUAL HELP

O Mother of Perpetual Help, grant that I may ever invoke your most powerful name, which is the safeguard of the living and the salvation of the dying. O Purest Mary, O Sweetest Mary, let your name henceforth be ever on my lips. Delay not, O Blessed Lady, to help me whenever I call on you, for, in all my needs, in all my temptations, I shall never cease to call on you, ever repeating your sacred name, Mary, Mary. O what consolation, what sweetness, what confidence, what emotion fill my soul when I pronounce your sacred name, or even only think of you. I thank God for having given you, for my good, so sweet, so powerful, so lovely a name. But I will not be content with merely pronouncing your name; let my love for you prompt me ever to hail you, Mother of Perpetual Help. Amen.